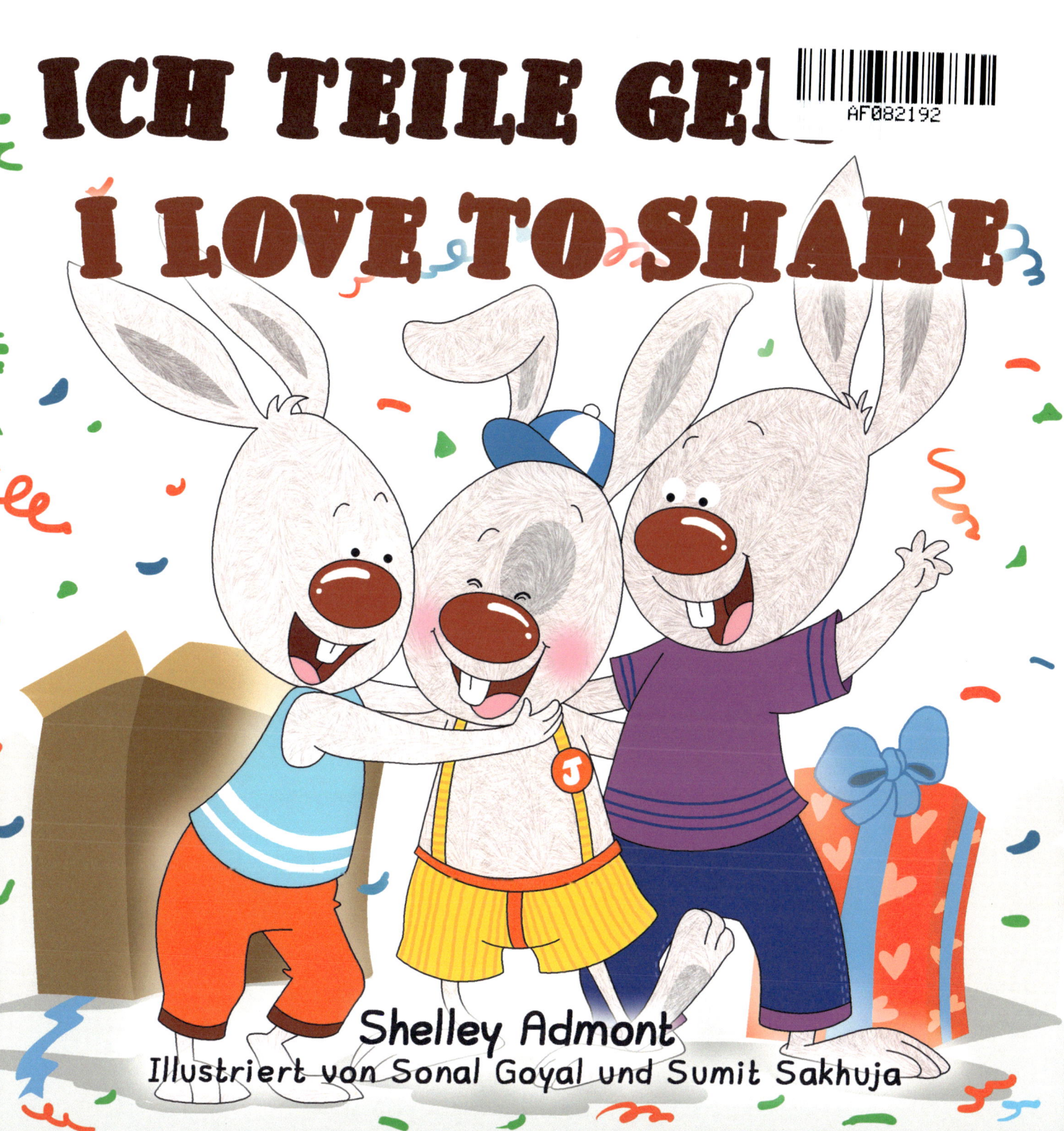

www.kidkiddos.com
Copyright©2015 by S.A.Publishing ©2017 by KidKiddos Books Ltd.
support@kidkiddos.com
All rights reserved. No part of this book may be reproduced in any form or by any electronic or mechanical means, including information storage and retrieval systems, without written permission from the publisher or author, except in the case of a reviewer, who may quote brief passages embodied in critical articles or in a review.
First edition, 2016

Translated from English by Tess Parthum
Aus dem Englischen übersetzt von Tess Parthum

Library and Archives Canada Cataloguing in Publication
I love to Share (German English Bilingual Edition)/ Shelley Admont
ISBN: 978-1-77268-226-7 paperback
ISBN: 978-1-77268-585-5 hardcover
ISBN: 978-1-77268-225-0 ebook

Please note that the German and English versions of the story have been written to be as close as possible. However, in some cases they differ in order to accommodate nuances and fluidity of each language.

Für die, die ich am meisten liebe-S.A.
For those I love the most-S.A.

„Schaut, wie viele neue Spielsachen ich habe!", sagte Jimmy, der kleine Hase, und sah sich im Zimmer um.

"Look at how many new toys I have," said Jimmy the little bunny, looking around the room.

Seine Geburtstagsparty war vorbei und das Zimmer war voller Geschenke.

His birthday party was over and the room was full of presents.

„Oh, deine Geburtstagsparty hat so viel Spaß gemacht, Jimmy", sagte sein mittlerer Bruder.

"Oh, your birthday party was so fun, Jimmy," his middle brother said.

„Lasst uns spielen!", sagte sein ältester Bruder. Er nahm die größte Schachtel. „Da ist ein riesiger Zug drin!"

"Let's play," said his oldest brother. He took the largest box. "There's a huge train inside!"

Plötzlich sprang Jimmy auf und griff nach der Schachtel. „Fass das nicht an! Es ist mein Zug!", rief er. „Diese Geschenke gehören alle MIR!"

Suddenly, Jimmy jumped to his feet and grabbed the box. "Don't touch it! It's my train!" he cried. "All these presents are **MINE!**"

„Aber Jimmy", sagte der älteste Bruder, „wir spielen immer zusammen. Was ist heute mit dir los?"

"But, Jimmy," said the oldest brother, "we always play together. What happened to you today?"

„Heute ist MEIN Geburtstag. Und das sind MEINE Spielsachen!", schrie Jimmy.

"Today is MY birthday. And these are MY toys," Jimmy screamed.

„Wir gehen lieber Basketball spielen", sagte der älteste Bruder. Er warf einen Blick aus dem Fenster. „Es ist schön und sonnig heute."

The oldest brother glanced out the window. "We better go play basketball," he said. It's nice and sunny today."

Die beiden Hasenbrüder nahmen einen Ball und gingen hinaus. Jimmy blieb alleine im Zimmer.

The two bunny brothers took a ball and went outside. Jimmy stayed in the room on his own.

„Ja!", rief er. „Jetzt sind alle Spielzeuge nur für mich!"

"Yeah!" he exclaimed. "Now all the toys are for me!"

Er nahm eine große Schachtel und öffnete sie glücklich. Darin fand er Bahngleise und einen neuen bunten Zug. Er musste nur die Schienen zusammensetzen.

He took a large box and opened it happily. Inside he found a rail trail and a new colorful train. He just needed to put the rail trail together.

„Oh, diese Teile sind zu klein!", sagte er, als er die Teile der Bahngleise nahm. „Wie soll ich sie miteinander verbinden?"

"Oh, these pieces are too small!" he said, holding the rail trail parts. "How should I connect them together?"

Er baute die Bahngleise zusammen, aber sie wurde schief. Als er schließlich seinen neuen bunten Zug anschaltete, blieb er auf der Strecke stecken.

Somehow he built the rail line, but it came out crooked. When he finally turned on his new colorful train, it got stuck on the track.

Jimmy sah sich um und entdeckte eine andere Schachtel.

Jimmy looked around and spotted another box.

„Kein Problem, ich habe noch mehr neue Spielzeuge", sagte er und nahm ein anderes Geschenk. Darin waren Superhelden-Figuren.

"No worries. I have more new toys," he said and took another present. Inside there were superhero toys.

„Toll!", rief Jimmy. Er fing an, mit den neuen Superhelden-Figuren in der Hand im Zimmer herumzurennen.

"Wow!" exclaimed Jimmy. He started to run around the room with new superhero toys in his hands.

Bald wurde er müde und langweilte sich. Er versuchte alles. Er spielte mit seinem Lieblings-Teddybär und er öffnete sogar alle seine Geschenke, aber es machte überhaupt keinen Spaß.

Soon he became tired and bored. He tried everything. He played with his favorite teddy bear and he even opened all his presents, but it was not fun at all.

Jimmy schaute aus dem Fenster und sah seine Brüder vergnügt mit ihrem Basketball spielen. Die Sonne schien hell und sie lachten und amüsierten sich.

Jimmy watched through the window and saw his brothers playing cheerfully with their basketball. The sun was shining brightly, and they were laughing and enjoying themselves.

„Wie können sie so viel Spaß haben? Sie haben nur einen Basketball!", sagte Jimmy. „All die anderen Spielsachen sind hier bei mir."

"How are they having so much fun? They only have one basketball!" said Jimmy. "All the other toys are here with me."

Dann hörte er eine fremde Stimme.

Then he heard a strange voice.

„Sie TEILEN", sagte sie.

"They SHARE," it said.

Jimmy sah sich im Zimmer um und starrte auf sein Bett, wo sein Teddybär saß. Die Stimme kam von dort.

Jimmy looked around the room, staring at his bed where his teddy bear sat. The voice came from *there*.

„Was?", flüsterte er.

"What?" he whispered.

„Sie teilen", wiederholte sein Teddybär mit einem Lächeln.

"They share," repeated his teddy bear with a smile.

Jimmy sah ihn erstaunt an. Er hatte nie gedacht, dass Teilen Spaß machen könnte.

Jimmy looked at him amazed. He never thought that sharing could be fun.

Jimmy schüttelte den Kopf. „Nein ... ich teile nicht gern. Ich liebe meine Spielzeuge."

Jimmy shook his head. "No…I don't like to share. I love my toys."

Inzwischen änderte sich das Wetter. Dunkle Wolken bedeckten den Himmel und große Regentropfen begannen, auf den Boden zu fallen.

Meanwhile the weather changed. Dark clouds covered the sky and large raindrops started falling to the ground.

Lachend rannten die zwei Hasenbrüder ins Haus.

Laughing, the two bunny brothers ran into the house.

„Oh, ihr seid ganz nass", sagte Mama. „Geht euch umziehen und ich werde euch heiße Schokolade machen."

"Oh, you're all wet," said Mom. "Go change your clothes and I'll make you hot chocolate."

„Komm, Jimmy, möchtest du auch heiße Schokolade?", fragte sie. Jimmy nickte.

"Come, Jimmy, do you want hot chocolate too?" she asked. Jimmy nodded.

Mama öffnete den Kühlschrank, um die Milch herauszunehmen. „Schau, da ist ein kleines Stück von deinem Geburtstagskuchen übrig."

Mom opened the fridge to grab the milk. "Look, there's a small piece of your birthday cake left," she said.

Jimmy sprang auf seine Füße. „Ja, kann ich es haben? Er war so lecker!"

Jimmy jumped to his feet. "Yeah, can I have it? It was so tasty!"

In diesem Augenblick kamen seine Brüder in die Küche.

At that moment, his brothers entered the kitchen.

„Hast du Kuchen gesagt?", fragte der mittlere Bruder.

"Did you say cake?" asked the middle brother.

„Ich hätte gerne ein Stück", fügte der älteste Bruder hinzu.

"I'd like a piece," added the oldest brother.

Ihr Vater folgte ihnen. „Ist das ein … Geburtstagskuchen?"

Their father followed them. "Is this a…birthday cake?"

Mama lächelte sanft. „Ähm … es ist eigentlich nur ein winzig kleines Stück übrig. Und wir sind zu fünft."

Mom smiled softly. "Ahh…there is actually a tiny little piece left. And there are five of us."

Jimmy schaute seine liebevolle Familie an und fühlte, wie sich ein warmes Gefühl von seinem Herzen aus ausbreitete. Er wusste, was er tun musste, und es fühlte sich so gut an.

Jimmy looked at his loving family and felt a warm feeling spread from his heart. He knew what he needed to do and it felt so good.

„Wir können teilen", sagte er. „Lasst es uns in fünf Stücke schneiden."

"We can share," he said. "Let's cut it into five pieces."

Alle Mitglieder der Hasenfamilie nickten. Dann setzten sie sich um den Tisch herum und alle genossen ein Stück Geburtstagskuchen und eine heiße Schokolade.

All the members of the bunny family nodded their heads. Then they sat around the table and everyone enjoyed a piece of birthday cake and a hot chocolate.

Jimmy warf einen Blick in ihre lächelnden Gesichter und dachte: Teilen kann sich also tatsächlich sehr gut anfühlen.

Jimmy glanced at their smiling faces and thought, *Sharing can actually feel very nice after all.*

Als sie fertig waren, kam Mama zu Jimmy und gab ihm eine große Umarmung. „Alles Gute zum Geburtstag, Schatz", sagte sie.

When they finished, Mom came to Jimmy and gave him a huge hug. "Happy birthday, honey," she said.

Die beiden älteren Brüder und ihr Vater versammelten sich um sie und stimmten in die Familienumarmung mit ein.

The two older brothers and their dad gathered around them and shared the family hug.

„Alles Gute zum Geburtstag, Jimmy", riefen sie zusammen.

"Happy birthday, Jimmy," they screamed together.

Jimmy lächelte. „Wollt ihr mit meinen Spielsachen spielen?", fragte er seine Brüder. „Ich habe einen neuen Zug und neue Superhelden."

Jimmy smiled. "Do you want to play with my toys?" he asked his brothers. "I have a new train and new superheroes."

„Jaaa! Lasst uns spielen!", schrien die Hasenbrüder.

"Yeah! Let's play!" shouted the bunny brothers.

Zusammen bauten Jimmy und seine Brüder eine perfekte Bahnstrecke. Der Zug pfiff und fuhr schnell auf den Gleisen umher.

Together Jimmy and his brothers built a perfect rail trail. The train whistled and ran fast around the track.

Dann öffneten sie die Geschenke und spielten mit all ihren Spielsachen.

Then they opened the presents and played with all their toys.

Von da an liebte es Jimmy zu teilen. Er sagte sogar, dass Teilen Spaß macht!

From then on, Jimmy loved to share. He even said that sharing is fun!

Made in the USA
Monee, IL
04 May 2026